Seattle World School
Seattle, Washington

THOMAS ALVA
EDISON

American Inventor and Businessman

Ellen M. Dolan

Enslow Publishers, Inc.
40 Industrial Road
Box 398
Berkeley Heights, NJ 07922
USA
http://www.enslow.com

Dedication

We wish to dedicate this book to the memory of Ellen M. Dolan.

Library of Congress Cataloging-in-Publication Data
Dolan, Ellen M., author.
  Thomas Alva Edison : American inventor and businessman / Ellen M. Dolan.
    pages cm. — (Legendary American biographies)
  "Originally published as: Thomas Alva Edison: Inventor," in 1998.
  Audience: Grades 4 to 6.
  Includes bibliographical references and index.
  ISBN 978-0-7660-6510-9
  1. Edison, Thomas A. (Thomas Alva), 1847–1931—Juvenile literature. 2. Inventors—United
States—Biography—Juvenile literature. 3. Scientists—United States—Biography—Juvenile
literature. I. Title.
  TK140.E3D75 2015
  621.3'092—dc23
                              2014029309
Future Editions:
Paperback ISBN: 978-0-7660-6511-6
EPUB ISBN: 978-0-7660-6512-3
Single-User PDF ISBN: 978-0-7660-6513-0
Multi-User PDF ISBN: 978-0-7660-6514-7

Printed in the United States of America
102014 Bang Printing, Brainerd, Minn.
10 9 8 7 6 5 4 3 2 1

To Our Readers: We have done our best to make sure all Internet addresses in this book were
active and appropriate when we went to press. However, the author and the publisher have no
control over and assume no liability for the material available on those Internet sites or on other
Web sites they may link to. Any comments or suggestions can be sent by e-mail to comments@
enslow.com or to the address on the back cover.

♻ Enslow Publishers, Inc., is committed to printing our books on recycled paper. The paper in
every book contains 10% to 30% post-consumer waste (PCW). The cover board on the outside
of each book contains 100% PCW. Our goal is to do our part to help young people and the
environment too!

Illustration Credits: © Enslow Publishers, Inc., p. 9; Library of Congress, p. 4;
Shutterstock.com: ©A-R-T (scrolls)

Cover Illustration: Library of Congress

CONTENTS

Thomas Alva Edison

Chapter 1

THE BIRTH OF ELECTRIC LIGHT

By 1878, Thomas Alva Edison was already a respected inventor, always hard at work trying to find ways to make life easier for families and businesses. In late August, he and other scientists had just returned from Wyoming and other western states, where they had journeyed to observe a solar eclipse. There, they had relaxed around a campfire and talked about their work. One of the scientists, George F. Barker, was familiar with Edison's work and encouraged Edison to experiment with a new idea.

Barker and Edison discussed the possibility of making electric light available for homes and businesses. At the time, fireplaces, candles, oil lamps, and lanterns were the usual ways to light a home. Bedcovers and drapes often caught fire when a candle accidentally touched them. Gas lamps along the streets provided such poor lighting that many city dwellers stayed home after dark.

Arc lighting was already in use, but it was not very practical for a home. Sir Humphry Davy, an English chemist, had created the arc lighting system, in which metal rods would glow when an electric current, or "arc," passed through the air around them. Arc lights were used primarily outdoors because they gave off dangerous sparks, made loud hissing noises, and produced an extremely bright light. Glowing with the brilliance of four thousand candles, arc lights were far too intense to be used indoors. They also tended to burn out within a few hours, making them too expensive for household use.[1] Edison wanted to design lighting with a softer glow, powered by electricity, that could be used by everyone. After returning from his trip, Edison went right to work.

Inventing the Lightbulb

While working on earlier inventions, Edison had experimented with batteries as a source of power. This idea, calling for the use of electricity, was a new and interesting experiment. He began working on a way to make a practical, inexpensive system of electric lighting. Edison had to find a way to set up a vast system of electric generators to provide the power for the lightbulbs he envisioned. He also faced other difficulties in making the experiment work. One of the biggest problems Edison faced in the months that he and his employees worked on the idea of the electric lightbulb was finding a filament—wick material or thin wire—that would allow the lightbulb to glow without breaking and that could withstand fierce heat.

Edison took this problem to his laboratory. He and his chief workers began to experiment. First, they needed a glass bulb strong enough to withstand heat without breaking. Then, they had to pump the air from the bulb, creating a vacuum, and insert a strong filament that would glow. The glassblowers made several bulbs and put them aside to cool. The bulbs were not all the same shape or size, but Edison did not think that was important.

Arc Lighting

Discovered around 1808 by the English chemist Sir Humphry Davy, arc lighting was one of the earliest methods of using electricity to provide a source of light. It worked by creating an arc of very strong heat and light, which occurred when an electric current was passed through a gap between metal strips, or electrodes. Though the arc system was later widely replaced by the much more convenient electric lightbulb, electric arcs are still used today for arc welding, searchlights, large film projectors, and in some experiments with nuclear particles.

Then, Edison had to come up with just the right filament. He tried many slender strands of various metals. Among them were expensive and unusual ones like platinum and chromium. Other experimental samples were much more ordinary. Edison even tried a bit of fishing line and some mustache hair. None of them worked. Each time, the filament quickly melted, and the light was extinguished. Although Edison's eyes were beginning to bother him from days and hours of constantly staring at tiny filaments inside glass bulbs, he would not give up. He was determined to find the answer to the problem. Again and again he went back to his lab table.[2]

Though many historians dispute it, according to his own version of the story, Edison had picked up a glass chimney from a gas lamp while searching for just the right filament. He saw the black sootlike material inside the glass and rubbed some of it off. Rolling it between his fingers, Edison began to wonder if this soot, or carbon, would ignite.[3] Applying the carbon to a piece of thread to use as a filament finally seemed to be a possible answer.

A bit of cotton sewing thread was slowly heated in a vacuum, making it "carbonized." Edison decided to try this thread, which had turned to carbon, as a filament. The thread was fragile, and the workers had to be very careful not to break it while trying to position it inside the bulb. Edison carefully placed the thread filament inside the glass bulb. He then removed the air from the bulb and sealed it. The tighter the vacuum was sealed, the longer the filament would burn.

The Lightbulb Is Born

On October 22, 1879, all the hard work finally paid off. The workers gathered around the table. Edison turned on the power. Not only did the filament glow, but according to a reporter for the New York *Herald*, its light lasted for thirteen and a half hours.[4]

The Edison lightbulb

The experiment was successful! The electric lightbulb was on its way to becoming a part of everyday life![5]

In December 1879, Edison invited scientists, friends and dignitaries to his lab in Menlo Park, New Jersey. There, Edison gave a demonstration of his new invention, the lightbulb. As word spread like wildfire to the general public, Edison's lab was overwhelmed by visitors, who flocked to see the new type of lighting that would forever change the way people lived and did business. They lined up for blocks and waited patiently to see this marvelous invention. Because Thomas Edison had tried hard to keep the details of his experiment from the press while still trying to make it work just right, many newspaper reporters had predicted his invention a failure. Now these very same newspaper reporters were pushing their way up to the lab doors for just a glimpse of the amazing electric light, and perhaps a word or two from the man they called the "Wizard of Menlo Park," the inventor Thomas Alva Edison.

As Edison presented his lightbulb to the world, scientists, newspaper reporters and ordinary people everywhere thought that—once again—Thomas Edison had worked a miracle!

Chapter 2

AN AMBITIOUS
CHILDHOOD

Young Thomas Edison had a long connection with Canada. His mother, Nancy Elliott, was born in Chenango County, New York, but grew up in Canada. Her father was a minister who believed that girls as well as boys should be educated. This was an unusual and quite enlightened view in the early 1800s. Nancy went to school and later became a teacher. In 1828, she married Samuel Edison, who was born in Ontario, Canada. Their first four children—Marion, William Pitt, Harriet, and Carlisle—were born in Canada.[1]

Samuel Edison: Canadian Rebel

In 1837, Samuel Edison joined the Canadian Rebellion, hoping to reform the government. At the time of this uprising, Canada was still a colony of Great Britain. Like the colonists in the American Revolution, Canadian rebels wanted to overthrow the British colonial government and set up their own government. The rebels, Samuel Edison among them, were idealistic. They hoped to create a government more closely linked to the people than the one controlled by the British, far away overseas. The rebels considered the American government under President Andrew Jackson to be a solid example of a good, working democracy. Their ultimate goal was to establish an American-style democracy in Canada. The British, however, put down the rebellion, and the rebel leaders had to flee or face punishment. Samuel Edison knew that he could not safely return home. He fled south about eighty miles and crossed the border into the United States at Port Huron, Michigan, hoping to escape punishment and to find a new home for his growing family.

A New Home in Ohio

A canal between the Huron River and Lake Erie had been recently constructed near Milan, Ohio. Samuel Edison heard that because of the canal, the town of Milan was growing quickly, and he decided to settle there.[2] As Edison went to work setting up a home in the community, one of his new American friends, Alva Bradley, the captain of a riverboat, carried letters back and forth between Samuel and Nancy Edison.

While in Milan, Edison soon realized that many buildings would be needed as the town grew. With a loan from Bradley, Edison opened a lumberyard and a shingle mill. Both businesses became successful, and Edison was able to begin planning a home for his family. For $220, Edison bought a plot of land overlooking the Huron River and the nearby canal. He built a brick house with leaded windows, white shutters, and a picket fence. The finished house fit well into the landscape of Milan, which was beginning to look like a New England village. Within a year the house was finished, and Edison sent for his wife and children to join him.

It was in this house in Milan, Ohio, that Thomas Alva Edison was born on February 11, 1847. He was the seventh and last child of Samuel and Nancy Edison. Three of the Edisons' youngest children had died, so Thomas grew up with an older brother and two sisters. His middle name was chosen to honor the family friend, Captain Alva Bradley. Everyone called young Thomas "Al."

When he was first born, he was weak and had an extremely large head. The doctor who delivered him thought that he might possibly be infected with "brain fever."[3] Young Thomas Edison, however, went on to survive the unusual ailment and became an active, intelligent child.

A Curious Child

From the beginning, Al was a curious boy—always asking questions and wondering how things worked. There is little definite information about Al's childhood, other than stories that have been passed down through the Edison family. According to these family legends, Al pulled out chicken feathers just to see what kept them in place. He captured ducks and studied their webbed feet. He was interested in how the family's goose hatched eggs.[4] One story tells how, one day when Al was about two years old, a family member found him sitting on a pile of goose eggs in the barn. He believed that if a chicken could hatch its eggs by sitting on them, he could probably hatch the goose's eggs himself.[5]

Occasionally, young Al's desire to understand the world around him got him into trouble. Day after day wagons loaded with wheat arrived in Milan. Farmers lined up along the wharf and waited to load their wheat onto boats for shipping up the canal to eastern ports. The wheat often arrived faster than it could be shipped, so a good bit was stored in Samuel Edison's grain elevators.

When Al was three years old, he wandered down to his father's grain elevators. Wanting to know what was inside the strange buildings, Al climbed an outside ladder to the top and looked down into the bin. Suddenly he lost his balance and fell forward into the wheat. Fortunately his father saw him fall and was able to rescue him before he was smothered under the pile of grain.

Al was not always so lucky, however. A few years later he was playing in his father's barn and decided to build a fire, hoping, as many children have done, to satisfy his curiosity about the hot flames. He gathered a pile of straw and lit it with a match. The fire spread rapidly and burned the entire barn to the ground.[6] The next day Al's father marched him into the town square and whipped him in front of the townspeople. In spite of this humiliating public punishment, Al continued to be curious about the many things he saw around him.

When Al was seven years old, there was another major change in his life. The owners of the Cleveland and Ohio Railroad wanted to build their tracks through Milan. The town leaders, however, did not want the smoke and noise the railroad would bring, and they also wanted to protect the thriving canal trade that had made the town prosper. For these reasons, they refused the request. It turned out to be a big mistake.

The railroad bypassed Milan and ran instead through Newark, Ohio, and on to Toledo. Shipping by train was much faster than by canal boats. Within a few years, as trains became the more popular and faster way to ship goods and people from place to place, Milan lost 80 percent of its population, and the deserted canal became a muddy mess.[7]

Moving to Port Huron

Although Al's father had built his own business and had become prosperous in Milan, he soon realized that he had no choice but

Public Whipping

In the mid-nineteenth century during Edison's youth, public whipping was a widely used form of punishment. A child who misbehaved would be brought to a public place and whipped by his or her parent or guardian in plain view of the townspeople. The practice was intended to encourage those who witnessed the whipping to behave better and to help prevent future misbehavior by reminding children of what they had done wrong.

to leave and find a new home for his family. In 1854, the Edison family traveled north, first by train and then by paddleboat, up the St. Claire River. Port Huron, Michigan, about one hundred miles north of Milan, was their destination.

The Edisons' new Michigan home was a large house surrounded by trees. It had six bedrooms, a big kitchen, and a handsome parlor. It was the storage cellar, however, that eventually became the most important room to Al. He would later conduct his first experiments there.

Although he was certainly energetic, Al was never very healthy as a child. The same year the Edisons moved to Port Huron, when Al was seven years old, he came down with scarlet fever. After that, he suffered frequently with colds and respiratory problems. Over the next few years, he began to notice problems with his hearing. His hearing would continue to deteriorate until, as an adult, he would be almost completely deaf. Many historians have guessed that his hearing loss was caused by fluid retained in his middle ear during one of his frequent childhood illnesses. However, the cause of the disability will probably never be known for certain.

A Hard-working Student

When he was eight years old, Al started school. He was eager to learn everything and asked question after question. As Edison later recalled (though many historians find the story doubtful), the man who ran the school did not like to be questioned. He was accustomed to quiet, obedient students, not those like the dreamy, easily distracted Edison. Edison said that the teacher made fun of him in front of the rest of the class, saying that Al must be "addled" (confused). Al's mother was so angry when she heard this that she decided to teach Al herself at home.[8]

Al learned quickly. Although he did not care much for math, he was immediately drawn to science. He was especially interested in a book called *A School Compendium of Natural and Experimental Philosophy* by R. G. Parker, which his mother gave him. Al's father also encouraged him to read and gave him a penny for every book he finished. Al worked his way through such difficult works as *The Age of Reason* by Thomas Paine. This book especially inspired him. Throughout his life, he would reflect on "the flash of enlightenment" the book brought him.[9] Though he had no further formal schooling, he developed an appetite for reading and eventually became self-educated.

Ending his formal education by the age of ten may sound unusual, but in the mid-nineteenth century, it was quite common. In fact, in the frontier lands of the Midwest, where Thomas Edison grew up, few children were educated past the age of ten. Those who were generally attended school only during the winter months when there was little work to be done around the family farm. However, Al was different from many of the children of his time; he tried hard to continue learning about everything around him long past the time when his years of formal schooling came to an end.

Early Experiments

When he was ten years old, Al got permission to set up a laboratory in the storage cellar beneath his house. Among the jars of canned fruit, vegetables, and dried corn, Al put in a chair, a table, and a few shelves.[10] Michael Oates, a teenage boy who had been hired to help the Edison family, was very interested in Al's work. As the two boys worked together caring for the Edisons' cows, chickens, and geese, Al explained to Michael that he wanted to conduct experiments in his new laboratory.

The two boys collected empty bottles and washed them carefully. Every Saturday Al took the pennies he had earned from reading and visited a chemist's shop in town. Among the items to be used in his private laboratory, he bought mercury to make a thermometer. That went into a bottle. Little by little Al filled dozens of bottles. Some held ordinary household materials like sugar or salt, but Al carefully labeled them all "Poison" and drew a skull and crossbones symbol under the word. Although Al knew what was in each bottle, he did not want anyone else to disturb his experiments.[11]

Al also collected scraps of wire and metal for his lab. Soon he learned about magnets and began to understand chemistry. Again and again he read Parker's *School Compendium*, an elementary physics textbook filled with experiments for students to conduct. Al tried every experiment suggested in the book and then began to try some of his own. One of Al's first experiments was with Seidlitz powder, which forms a gas when mixed with liquid. Al had heard that a gas-filled balloon would rise. He reasoned that if Michael drank plenty of the liquid mixture, enough gas would form in his stomach to lift him off the ground and allow him to fly. Poor Michael did not rise an inch into the air, but he did get very sick.[12] After that, Al's father locked up the laboratory, and there were no more experiments for several months.

Discovering the Telegraph

Since he could no longer conduct experiments, Al turned back to his books and began to study electricity. He had already noticed that when lightning flashed across the fields, several seconds passed before the accompanying thunder could be heard. He also learned that electricity was the power source for the telegraph system, which allowed people from different towns to send messages to one another by using the dots and dashes of Morse code.

Samuel F. B. Morse had invented the telegraph in 1832. It was a system that allowed people to communicate over a distance through clicking sounds produced by a series of electrical pulses that could be sent over wires by pushing down a telegraph key. Depending on its length, the pulse would be called a dot or a dash (with the dash being three times as long as the dot). Morse created a code of dots and dashes that stood for the letters of the alphabet and numerals. For the first time people who were far away from one another could communicate almost instantly.

Al was eleven years old when he and a friend, Jim Clancy, decided to try making their own telegraph system. They wanted to send messages back and forth between their homes, which were about half a mile apart. First, they gathered several empty bottles and broke off their necks. They slid nails through the open necks to fasten them to trees and fence posts along the road between the two houses. Then, they wound wire around the smooth outside of each neck and stretched it between the two houses. All they needed were batteries to provide the electricity to make the system work.

Instead of using batteries, Al thought of another way to generate electricity. He had noticed that the fur of cats often crackled with static electricity. Perhaps he could harness that electricity and use it at his sending station. Al found two cats, rubbed their tails together, and tried to attach them to his station. The cats yowled, spat, and scratched.[13] Reluctantly, Al let them go and decided to use battery power instead. He connected the batteries and tapped out his first Morse code message: "Hello."

First Job

In 1859 the railroad came to Port Huron, creating much excitement. At age twelve, Al persuaded his parents to let him start working. Like many young people of his time, he already felt a strong desire to strike out on his own—to earn money for himself and his family. The Grand Trunk Railroad had extended its line from Toronto, Canada, to Port Huron, and then farther

Morse Code

Invented by Samuel F. B. Morse, Morse code became the standard "language" used in transmitting telegraph messages. The dot and dash symbols, sent by short or long pulses of electrical current across the telegraph wire, represent the letters of the alphabet, as shown in this diagram:

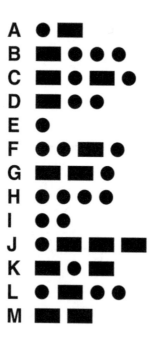

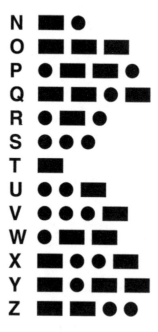

south to Detroit. Al got a job selling newspapers to travelers on the railroad from his hometown to Detroit and back. Soon he added fruit and candy to his inventory. Each day Al proudly gave his mother one dollar—almost all his earnings.

It was a long workday for Al. He got up just before dawn to catch the 7:00 A.M. train for Detroit and did not return home to Port Huron until 9:30 P.M. The so-called mixed train on which he worked carried passengers as well as freight. To make better use of his free time on board the train, Al persuaded a conductor to let him set up a laboratory in the baggage car, which was rarely full. With chemicals from his basement lab at home, Al began some experiments.

At first, it seemed like a good arrangement. Then, one of the experiments backfired. A bottle of phosphorus rolled off the table, crashed to the floor, and set the baggage car on fire. Al quickly smothered the flames. The fire had caused no major damage, but the angry conductor threw all of the chemicals—and Al—off the train. Al was in trouble for a while, but soon returned to work.[14]

Working on the railroad gave Al many opportunities he would not have had at home. Each workday there was a five-hour layover in Detroit before the train's return trip to Port Huron. The city of Detroit was ten times the size of Port Huron, and Al took advantage of its sights. He spent part of each afternoon in the library of the Young Men's Society (later the Detroit Public Library), reading, learning, and thinking. Then he purchased the newspapers and produce he would sell on the trip home.

When Al was in Detroit, he often visited with the staff at the *Detroit Free Press*. He checked to see what the major newspaper stories of the day would be. Al then calculated how many papers he might sell on his route, based on his observations of his customers' interests. One day he learned that news of the Civil War battle at Shiloh, Tennessee, was just off the press. Realizing that the progress of the Civil War was of major interest to readers and that this bloody battle was a very important event in a conflict that could change the lives of Americans everywhere, Al ordered many more papers than usual. On previous trips Al had made friends in the telegraph offices along the railroad line. He wired ahead to the offices to let them know he was bringing firsthand news of the battle.

His friends spread the word. At the train's first stop, a crowd, clamoring for the news, was already waiting for Al and his newspapers. Already a keen businessman, Al realized that this was a good opportunity to earn a bit more money than usual. He raised the price of the paper from two cents to ten cents. As the train moved on to the Mount Clemens stop, Al saw that more customers were waiting. Seeing their eagerness for the latest news from the battlefront, Al raised the price of his papers to fifteen cents. As the train approached the station at Port Huron, a large crowd had again gathered to wait for the news. When Al saw this, he immediately raised his price to the enormous sum of twenty-five cents. Even in his early years, Thomas Edison knew how to succeed in business!

The Young Businessman

Encouraged by his ability to make money with his skills and intelligence, Al continued to expand his business interests. He opened a stand in Port Huron where he sold vegetables as well as newspapers and hired other boys in town to help him.[15] He supplied them with newspapers, magazines, and fresh produce, which he bought from vendors in Detroit or at train stops on the way back to Port Huron.

Because of his experience selling papers and working with up-to-the-minute news reports, by 1862, Al understood the newspaper business fairly well. He began to put together his own publication, the weekly Grand Trunk *Herald*. He had the time to work on it during the long train trips. Each week his customers could read bits of international news, jokes, and lost-and-found notices. Knowing he would sell more papers if he catered to the special interests of his customers, Al also included railroad information such as the change of a timetable or the addition of a new stop on the line. He sold subscriptions to his paper for eight cents a month.

Al put in long days and many late nights on the railroad. Still, he continued to spend time in the evening "talking" to Jim Clancy on his homemade telegraph set. Little by little Al was able to practice sending and receiving simple messages. He was fascinated by this amazing invention that allowed people to communicate faster than any person or horse could carry a message.

By a stroke of luck and quick thinking, Al came upon an opportunity to improve his telegraph skills. One day at the Mount Clemens railroad stop, Al stepped off the train for a break. As he stood on the platform, he noticed a small child playing on the nearby tracks. A freight car was rolling down the tracks toward the little boy, who did not see it. Quickly Al snatched the boy out of the way—just in time.

The child was the son of James Mackenzie, a professional telegraph operator. As a reward, the grateful father gave Al free telegraph lessons. With Mackenzie's help, Al greatly improved his skills in sending and receiving messages by Morse code. It was the beginning of a new adventure for Al.[16]

Chapter 3

THE YOUNG
TELEGRAPHER

In 1862, when Thomas Edison began to seriously develop his skills as a telegraph operator, the Civil War was nearing the end of its first year. Telegraph messages were a vital tool for newspaper reporters as well as for the armies of both the North and the South. Telegraph operators were working long hours relaying news.

At the time, the telegraph system was still somewhat crude, and messages had to be sent in short relays. Sending a message from Boston, Massachusetts, to St. Louis, Missouri, required a chain of six operators working together to pass the signals from one telegraph station to the next.

Wartime Opportunity

Many skilled, experienced operators had gone to war and were at the front lines, working exclusively for the Union. So there was a scarcity of operators for local telegraph offices. Three months after Edison finished his training with James Mackenzie, the Port

Huron telegrapher resigned to join the telegraphers who were working on the Union front lines.

Fifteen-year-old Edison, whose skills were not yet fully developed, took over the job. The telegraph office was in a corner of Micah Walker's Port Huron book and jewelry store. The equipment consisted of a telegraph key, a register, and a set of batteries. Press reports came over the wires until 3 A.M., so Edison frequently slept at Walker's.

Edison enjoyed receiving and sending current national news. In spite of the hearing problem he had developed as a young child, he began to master the telegraph. When he missed parts of a message, he was able to fill in the gaps by guessing the appropriate words. He was not the only operator who did not fully catch each transmission. The dots and dashes of the Morse code were not always easy to make out clearly, and often any background noise made it especially hard to catch a message completely. Most operators had to use the "fill in the gaps" method in order to complete a full message. By continually reading newspapers to stay in touch with national events, operators like Edison were able to make sense out of incomplete messages. Edison kept up with all the latest news and practiced sending press reports again and again.

Traveling Telegrapher

By 1863, Edison's skills had become good enough for him to take a job as a telegrapher for the Grand Trunk Railroad in Stratford Junction, Ontario, Canada. He was now sixteen years old. This was the first in a series of jobs that would take him around Canada and the United States. It was at this job that Edison first developed what would become his habit of catching catnaps whenever possible, rather than settling down for a regular night's sleep. One night while he was on duty, Edison wanted to get a little sleep and made a deal with the night watchman to wake him if a train came through the station. Unfortunately the watchman failed to do so, and Edison was still asleep when a freight came through and two trains almost collided. Edison was fired for his mistake.

Next, he was hired for the night shift at Adrian, Michigan. While there, Edison was given an urgent telegraph message with instructions to send it through immediately, even if other messages had to be interrupted to do so. Edison followed the orders, perhaps a little too closely. One of the messages he interrupted while trying to get the message through was that of his supervisor. When Edison explained what had happened to the supervisor, the person who had given him the initial instructions denied having given the orders. As a result of this misunderstanding, Edison was fired once again.

After a brief stay in Toledo, Ohio, Edison spent two months at the Fort Wayne, Indiana, office of Western Union. There, he began to experiment with ways to make the mechanical telegraph signals work more smoothly. Edison was then transferred to the Western Union office in Cincinnati, Ohio, in February 1865. Cincinnati was one of the largest urban areas in the country. As a new employee, Edison usually worked the night shift, which was not as busy as the daytime shifts. During the day he had time to read and think about new experiments.

At that time, most telegraph operators across the United States were young, single men who could move easily from city to city. Edison fit into that category. He was basically a "loner" who spent little time caring about his clothing or appearance. Still, he managed to develop some lasting friendships with the other young operators.

Through 1865 Edison worked as a regular "press wire," or daytime operator, in Memphis, Tennessee. Then, he went to Western Union in Louisville, Kentucky, where he earned $110 per month and worked with sixteen other men.[1]

Western Union

One of the first telegraph companies in the United States, Western Union became the main provider of long-distance messages in the 1850s. Thomas Edison would later contribute to its success with some of his inventions and improvements on the telegraph. In the 1900s, the company began to send messages by radio beams, which were relayed by a system of towers. By the 1950s, Western Union introduced the telex system, a new way to send messages over phone lines. Western Union is still in operation today, providing money transfers and related services.

By 1866, Edison had become one of the fastest receivers in the telegraph business. He was dedicated to his work and did not mind that he and the other young operators often had to live in shabby places. He often encountered huge cockroaches and rickety furniture at various telegraph offices, but he paid little attention to either. He was far more interested in conducting experiments on building a duplex telegraph system, which would have the ability to send two messages at once over a single wire.[2]

Learning About the World

With the constant stream of news coming across the wires, Edison was always intensely aware of what was going on in national politics. He heard both sides in many debates and realized how quickly the business world was growing.

As a young man traveling widely throughout the North and the Midwest, Edison was bombarded with many of the issues facing the world of his time. During the years after the Union won the Civil War, Americans were debating ideas that would change the social structure of the United States forever. Among the issues that Edison heard about in his work and in his travels from telegraph station to telegraph station was the argument over the rights of women and whether women should be permitted to vote. Leaders like Elizabeth Cady Stanton and Susan B. Anthony were then just coming into prominence as leaders of the movement that would work to gain women's suffrage (the right to vote).

At the same time, many were debating the rights of African Americans. After the end of the Civil War, racial issues were still difficult and sensitive topics. Though Edison himself had been too young and too far removed in Michigan to be directly touched by the actual fighting of the war, he was still aware of the bitter disagreements over slavery and about the rights of the former slaves after the war was over. There was also controversy over moving American Indians onto reservations, lands set aside for them by the United States government, and the often cruel treatment the Indians received from the government.

Edison kept up with all these issues, reading the newspapers in order to be a more effective telegraph operator and because he was genuinely interested in learning all he could about the world around him. During his years of travel, Edison also continued his habit of reading widely in different subject areas in order to better educate himself. Among his favorite authors at this time were philosophers like Ralph Waldo Emerson and businessmen like Andrew Carnegie. Edison understood that to be successful himself, he would do well to become familiar with the ideas and suggestions of those who had succeeded in different areas.

Also during this time, Edison made plans with some friends to seek employment as telegraph operators in South America. The young men had heard that telegraph operators were needed in Brazil, where telegraphy was just being set up. Edison, as curious as ever about the world and its mysteries, thought it would be an exciting opportunity. He even began to learn Spanish in order to make the venture as successful as possible (even though Portuguese is actually Brazil's official language). The trip fell through, however, and Edison remained in the United States, continuing to find telegraph work wherever it was available.[3]

Eventually, he returned to the Western Union office in Cincinnati. Again he spent time in the local library, reading scientific and telegraphic journals. Many of them were filled with experiments.

Return to Port Huron

Though he enjoyed his work and was always busy trying to improve himself and his skills, Edison was becoming tired from the long hours and the poor food he ate. Late in 1867, he returned to Port Huron for a rest and a visit with his family. There had been many changes.

Early in the Civil War, Union soldiers had come to Port Huron and taken over the Edison home to use as a barracks. The house was later burned, and the family was forced to move to a smaller house. Edison's mother had been ill for some time, and his father was having financial troubles because of some failed business deals. The Edisons were taking in boarders to help meet expenses. It was sad for young Thomas Edison to see his parents' situation. He could remember the days when his father was a successful man with prosperous businesses. Still, Edison was glad to have a chance to rest and to visit with his family. Being at home, away from the tough work and late hours at the telegraph office, he was also able to catch up on his reading.

In 1868, Edison was twenty-one years old and eager to move on again. Since his family was having problems, he also knew he needed to earn some money not only to support himself but also to help his family. Milton Adams, a friend from Edison's days in Cincinnati, was then working in Boston for the Franklin Telegraph Company. He told Edison that the Boston branch of Western Union was looking for workers. If Edison would move to Boston, Adams promised to help him get a job.

Moving to Boston

Eager to be useful, Edison said good-bye to his family and boarded a train for Boston. The weather was miserable, and the train was frequently delayed by blizzards and snowdrifts. Finally, it arrived in Boston. Edison had no time to clean up before rushing to his interview with George Milliken, the manager of the Western Union office in Boston. Although he privately thought Edison's clothes and manner were "countrified," Milliken was extremely impressed with Edison's skills and hired the young man within five minutes.

At that time Boston was a big city with two telegraph companies. Western Union had four lines, and the Franklin Telegraph Company had three. Edison was very much impressed with his new job and with the city of Boston, a center not only for culture but also for scientific learning and technical know-how. Edison marveled at the number of informed men who were walking the streets and talking of science and inventions. Milton Adams helped Edison find a place to stay. His first home was a tiny bedroom tucked into the corner of a boardinghouse hallway. But he did not mind; he was in Boston, and he was starting a new adventure!

In spite of long working hours, Edison found time for his experiments. He pored over a book on electrical experiments by Michael Faraday, a well-known scientist who seemed to have a background and approach similar to that of Edison.[4] Both men had started out relatively poor, and both were driven toward the possibility of success by a spirit of self-improvement and a desire to constantly learn. Both would also eventually use their talent and passion for science to make products that would be of commercial value. Edison came to see Faraday as a role model.

First Invention

Within a short time, Edison had learned enough about electricity to start working on developing an electric vote recorder for the Washington, D.C., city council. He applied for a patent on it in 1868. Edison received his first patent—U.S. No. 90,646—in 1869.[5] (A patent is granted to an inventor by the government to give the inventor exclusive rights to an invention for a certain period of time—seventeen years in the United States. When a patent is issued, no one else is legally allowed to make, sell, or use the product made by the inventor without his or her permission.) Unfortunately, the recorder was not a big success. Politicians wanted the chance to bargain with fellow representatives and

George Milliken

As the manager of the Western Union branch in Boston, George Milliken hired Edison because of Edison's previous experience in dealing with reports from the press. Like Edison, Milliken had the instincts of an inventor. He improved the strength of the telegraph wire by using a steel core covered by copper. Milliken and Edison became good friends.

perhaps change their votes during a session. Once a vote was recorded on Edison's device, it would be very difficult to change.

Edison decided he would not spend time in the future working on projects that would serve no practical purpose. He realized that no matter how interesting and creative an invention was, people had to want to buy it in order for it to be a success. With the failure of his first big attempt to market a product he had invented, Edison learned a lesson that would stay with him throughout his career. From then on, he would always remember to combine good business sense with whatever scientific innovations he produced.

Not allowing himself to be discouraged by the failure of the vote recorder, Edison went ahead with his next venture—an automatic stock ticker. The machine would be installed in the offices of wealthy businessmen, who had to keep close track of market prices. Information on the current prices of stocks was necessary to help them make good investments.

Edison had rented rooms in Boston's business section, where he set up headquarters for his stock-quoting service. Because he had spent so much of the money he had earned from experiments for creating a duplex telegraph line, however, there was little money left for him to live on.

Full-time Inventor

While in Boston, Edison also took a dramatic step. He decided to stop working for different telegraph companies and go into business for himself—as a full-time inventor. He resigned from Western Union, putting out a newspaper ad that announced he was planning to devote all of his time to inventing. It was a big step, but, as usual, Edison was determined that he could make it on his own. He soon decided it was time to leave Boston and look for opportunities elsewhere.

Chapter 4

STARTING A CAREER AS AN INVENTOR

In 1869, four years after the end of the Civil War, Edison moved to New York City. The war had gone on for four long year, the conflict had cost a lot of money, and many people struggled to make ends meet.

The postwar inflation had left Edison in debt. Leaving his books and instruments behind in Boston to cover some of his debts, Edison arrived in New York, the center of the American telegraph industry, without much money or the right clothing. He was used to his modest lifestyle by now. Still, he knew it would be difficult to start all over again. Although he still wanted to be a full-time inventor, he knew the first thing he had to do, to get his life back on track, was to get a job.

Making a Living in New York

He went to see Franklin L. Pope, an electrical engineer with New York's Gold & Stock Reporting Telegraph Company. The company used the latest information on the current prices of gold to help its clients make profitable investments. The investors hoped to buy when prices were low and sell when they were high. Edison thought his skills and technical knowledge would be useful to the company. Pope was impressed with Edison's previous inventions and scientific background, but had no opening for him.

On the third day after his arrival in New York, Edison again tried to apply for a job with the company. While he waited for an interview, the gold ticker machine in the company's office broke down. Investors, who relied on the ticker's information, flooded the office with questions. What was wrong? Samuel Laws, the company supervisor, did not know what to do. Edison, who was in the office at the time, became aware of the problem. When he went to investigate, Edison saw that a spring had broken off and lodged in the machinery. He offered to repair the equipment. Within two hours, Edison had the ticker running again. Laws was impressed and offered Edison a job.[1]

Edison gratefully accepted the position,developing a better gold ticker machine. When his friend Pope left the company to form his own business, Edison got Pope's old job as head engineer of the Gold & Stock Reporting Telegraph Company.

While working at Gold & Stock, Edison succeeded in creating an improved gold ticker. Edison's new machine was much more efficient than the earlier model. In fact, it was so much better that Western Union officials bought the entire Gold & Stock Reporting Telegraph Company in 1871 in order to take advantage of the new technology.

A New Company

That fall, Edison decided to leave New York City for nearby Elizabeth, New Jersey, where he again joined forces with his friend Pope. Because Edison was now recognized in scientific circles as an inventor, the two decided to start their own business, making sure to include Edison's name in the company's title.

They formed "Pope, Edison, and Co." and registered patents on a new gold ticker as well as several improved telegraph systems.[2]

Marshall Lefferts, who had become the head of the Gold & Stock Reporting Telegraph Company in 1870, was trying to create a better stock indicator. It would serve much the same purpose as the gold indicator—bringing news of the latest stock prices to investors who could use it to make their business deals. Lefferts asked Edison to work on the stock ticker. Edison was somewhat reluctant, but he needed money to continue his work on other experiments. He was able to develop a more efficient indicator. When he presented the invention to Lefferts, Edison hoped that the improved machine would earn him a five-thousand-dollar check. Instead, Lefferts was so impressed with Edison's machine that he paid Edison forty thousand dollars for his work! Edison could hardly believe the huge amount of money he had just received, but he knew just what he was going to do with it. He would start his very own business, working on inventions and with the machines he loved.

The American Telegraph Works

Edison set up a new company in Newark, New Jersey. It was housed in a four-story brick building, nine miles from New York City. Edison planned to manufacture stock tickers for Western Union. His new company, the American Telegraph Works, was located just across the street from the Newark railroad station.

Thomas Edison hired fifty employees, both men and women, to work at the new company. Charles Batchelor, known as Batch, was Edison's first and most loyal worker. Batch was two years older than Edison and had the lab seat next to his boss. Among the other employees were John Ott, a machinist; John Kruesi, a clock maker from Switzerland; and Sigmund Bergmann, a mechanic from Germany. These four men would remain with Edison for many years to come.[3]

An Inventive Routine

Edison and his employees established a laboratory routine, which would someday become almost as famous as the inventions it helped produce. Like many other imaginative people, Edison most enjoyed the mental process involved in creating an idea for a project. While he enjoyed the hard work of finding the solution to a problem, he also accepted the help of his employees in trying to make one of his ideas come to life.

Whenever Edison came up with an idea for an invention that he wanted to experiment with, he would begin the creative process by making a sketch of his idea and sharing it with his assistants. The lab workers would then examine the sketch. Batch, who was a good draftsman, could usually understand what Edison had in mind and was able to work with Kruesi to turn the sketches into a workable machine. Through the combined efforts of all the lab workers over several weeks, a model was usually ready. The model would serve as the first example of how the finished invention would work.

Edison and his employees set to work, putting their routine to the test. In addition to the tickers that Edison had worked on earlier, there were many other ideas to explore. All sorts of small inventions were produced in the building. Much of the work centered on new ideas for precision metalworking and industry.

Edison was a hands-on employer, choosing to work side by side with his employees. Perhaps because he had become used to shabby clothing and a careless appearance during his days as a young telegraph operator, he did not care if he got oil and grime all over his clothes. He was also greatly interested in getting input from others about his ideas and how his inventions worked. He frequently asked his employees for their opinions and discussed new ideas with them. Because he had spent most of of his life in ordinary jobs around working-class people, Edison did not necessarily consider himself better than the others at his company just because he was the boss.

Of course, Edison understood that the workers had to have discipline and respect in order to get their jobs done each day. But he also recognized that a lively, comfortable atmosphere is important for employee happiness and morale. With his own clever sense of humor and easygoing attitude, Edison was able to create an environment in which those who worked for him could bring unusual or untried ideas to him without fear of being humiliated. Edison also loved practical jokes. If he caught one of the workers dozing, he pulled out what he called his "corpse reviver"—a huge rattle enclosed in a wooden box. Edison would turn the crank on the side of the box, creating a loud, grating sound. The sleepy worker would almost leap off his stool. After much good-natured laughter, the "revived" employee went back to work.

Because Edison worked alongside his employees, the place took on a feeling of camaraderie that was absent from most formal businesses of the time. In spite of his relative youth—just twenty-four years old—his employees began to affectionately call Edison "the Old Man."[4]

Love and Marriage

In 1871, the employees noticed that Edison was paying extra attention to a very pretty female employee at the News Reporting Telegraph Company, one of the branches of Edison's business. Her name was Mary Stilwell, and she was just sixteen years old. Mary had beautiful skin, long curly hair, and a lovely smile. She came from a large, middle-class family much like Edison's.

Soon, Edison was inviting Mary to music hall performances and buying her expensive presents. After dating for only about three months, Mary and Edison were making wedding plans. On an unusually warm Christmas Day in 1871, the two were married in a simple ceremony.[5]

Over the next few years, the young couple had three children—in 1873, a girl, named Marion Estelle, and two boys, Thomas Alva, Jr., in 1876 and William Leslie in 1878. When playing with the two eldest children, Edison nicknamed them "Dot" and "Dash." These were playful references to the dots and dashes of Morse code.[6]

A very private man, Edison kept his family life separate from his professional work. Although he generally enjoyed being with his family, work was always most important to Edison, and he continued to spend long hours in the lab. Time just slipped by when he became interested in a project. He spent so much time away from home, in fact, that his wife became somewhat unhappy.

Mary was, in general, a quiet person who kept mainly to herself except when she was around those she knew very well. She did everything she could to try to please her new husband. Edison, however, was not easily impressed by anything outside the sphere to which he had long been accustomed—science and technology. For the most part, Mary's efforts to make home life more satisfying for Thomas Edison went unnoticed. Over time she began to feel abandoned, especially as her husband grew more famous and spent even more time away from home.[7]

A Productive Inventor

All of Edison's hard work did not go unrewarded. In the first six months of 1872 alone, Edison registered thirteen patents, and his prestige as an inventor increased. In 1874, he invented the quadruplex, an improvement on his earlier duplex telegraph system. The duplex, which Edison had worked on while he was a telegraph operator but had not completed, sent two messages in the same direction simultaneously over one wire. The quadruplex system could send two messages in one direction and two more in the opposite direction at the same time over one wire.[8] This invention was a big improvement over the duplex system, greatly increasing the number of messages that could be handled by telegraph operators.

During this time Edison also invented an electric pen, which could duplicate human handwriting. The user held it just like an ordinary pen and wrote normally. But the electric pen had a needle that moved rapidly and made tiny holes in the paper, which could be filled with ink to make an exact copy of the original page. The invention would save people a lot of time—including Edison and his workers, who spent hours upon hours filling out multiple forms for patents and other business matters. It would allow them to write something only once, yet have the ability to make almost unlimited copies.

The Quadruplex

A vast improvement over previous telegraph technology, Edison's quadruplex was a multiple telegraph system that worked by combining a duplex circuit with the duplex telegraph system. A duplex circuit was a device that could send two messages in the same direction, whereas the duplex system could send two messages in opposite directions. Combining both of these components, the quadruplex gave the telegraph operator the ability to transmit four messages at one time, two in either direction. It was an enormous help in easing the telegrapher's workload.

These inventions made significant profits for Edison. Just two years later, in 1876, he was ready to expand his business again. Now that he had his own company and was enjoying his success as an inventor, he wanted a particular kind of workplace—a laboratory with enough room to do experiments as large as he pleased. He found just the right place and moved both his company and his family to Menlo Park, New Jersey.

Chapter 5

THE INVENTION FACTORY AT MENLO PARK

Menlo Park was a farming village about twelve miles south of Newark, New Jersey. It was about twenty-five miles from New York City and an easy train ride to Philadelphia, Pennsylvania. In early 1876, Edison began to build a large laboratory in Menlo Park. He asked his father, Samuel, to come from Port Huron and oversee the construction.

Menlo Park, New Jersey

There were several reasons for Edison's move. First, Menlo Park was in a remote area primarily devoted to agriculture, and the land was fairly cheap. Second, away from the crowded city and the bustle of everyday business, Edison and his employees would have the opportunity to work on their experiments in peace and quiet, without any interference from competing businesses or curious people. Finally, Menlo Park was in an ideal location for travel to the cities where major businesses were located, making it possible for Edison to leave his isolated laboratory to meet with fellow inventors or financial backers when necessary.

Menlo Park was designed according to Edison's own specifications. Edison wanted his new laboratory to be devoted exclusively to conducting experiments. Earlier laboratories were not like those of today. Rather than being devoted completely to researching and developing new ideas and inventions, laboratories then were more like workshops. That is, they combined invention with the real work of the company—making products that could be sold to customers for a profit.

Edison still wanted to make products that people would buy. But he also wanted to create a special work space where he and his employees could devote themselves entirely to coming up with innovative ideas and new, useful products, rather than spending their time putting together and trying to sell the products they made. The idea of a building to be used exclusively for experimenting with new products and ideas was unique. There were many scientists who later believed that this laboratory was Edison's best invention of all.

A New Kind of Laboratory

The Menlo Park laboratory was located in a two-story white frame building. A few small storage sheds were nearby. One of them was to be used only for experiments with carbon. The complex was surrounded by a white picket fence and included a brick office. On the second floor of the lab the walls were lined with over two thousand bottles of chemicals. The setup was a vast improvement over the basement laboratory Edison had created as a child in Port Huron. Instead of a random assortment of bottles labeled with skulls and crossbones, each vial at Menlo Park contained a specific chemical for a specific purpose. Throughout the laboratory, workstations were set at intervals down the middle of the building. In a separate building was the machine shop. Also kept there were earlier models of machinery and inventions that were not successful or that had become obsolete. When workers needed a part for a current experiment, they might find it there.[1]

Family Life and Visitors

The laboratory was also in a convenient place for enjoying the hours away from work. Edison bought a large home on nearby Christie Street for his family. A plank walk ran from the laboratory to the house. Edison persuaded a widow he knew, Sarah Jordan, to open a boardinghouse for the lab workers.[2] Each day Edison's oldest child, Marion, brought her father's lunch to the laboratory. Most of the time Edison remembered to eat it.

Visitors from foreign countries, as well as from various parts of the United States, came frequently to see Edison and his unique laboratory. James Mackenzie, who had first taught Edison telegraphy, visited often. Many journalists and dignitaries were also interested in the lab and came to see it. For overnight visitors, there were several boardinghouse rooms available. Before long there was also a small restaurant, which served lunch for thirty cents. Edison himself always planned to be home for dinner, especially when he knew he had company, but he often got caught up in the experiment at hand and stayed in the lab all through the night.

In the laboratory during these early years at Menlo Park, Edison continued to improve and modernize new models of the telegraph. He was also intrigued by the telephone.

Alexander Graham Bell and the Telephone

In 1876, Alexander Graham Bell patented the first telephone. Bell had become interested in the human voice while he was tutoring deaf children.

Edison viewed Bell's telephone as an extension of some of his own earlier work with telegraphy. Instead of sending the dots and dashes of Morse code, however, the telephone sent sound. In a sense, the telephone was also similar to the electric pen Edison had invented. The electric pen had the ability to duplicate human handwriting. The telephone did the same for the human voice.

Aside from his scientific interest in Bell's accomplishment, Edison was interested in working on the telephone for other reasons. Western Union urged Edison to start experimenting on ways to improve Bell's telephone. The huge telegraph company was quite concerned that the telephone could pose a threat to its own communications business and hoped that with improvements made by Edison, Western Union would be able to get around the patents issued to Bell and make money off the invention, too.

Edison's main goal in his work with the telephone was to try to improve the telephone's quality of sound. He thought the instrument could be made to sound better and louder. He also thought its design was awkward and difficult to use. When using the Bell telephone, the caller had to move a single device, which both sent and received sound, from the ear to the mouth,

Alexander Graham Bell

Born in Scotland, Alexander Graham Bell immigrated to Canada and then to the United States. Because both his mother and his future wife were deaf, Bell was greatly interested in helping the deaf learn to speak. His interest in the human voice and sound led to his invention of the telephone. On March 10, 1876, Bell made the first successful transmission of the human voice over the telephone.

depending on whether the caller was listening or talking to the person at the other end of the line. In addition, the power on which the telephone ran was, in Edison's opinion, insufficient. The sound could travel only about twenty miles.

In 1877, Edison improved the system by creating both a mouthpiece and an earpiece. This made using the telephone much less awkward. He also developed a transmitter that could carry messages over a much greater distance. These rather simple improvements earned Edison a quarter of a million dollars and added a great deal to his prestige.

The Invention of the Phonograph

Later in 1877, Edison thought more about the idea of transmitting a voice over a wire. Perhaps, he thought, it could be captured in some way so the sound could be kept permanently. This was the beginning of his development of the phonograph.

The invention of the phonograph came about when an accident occurred during Edison's usual laboratory routine. While working with one of their many telegraph projects, Edison and his workers put too much current through a motor, causing some discs they were experimenting with to fly around. The discs made contact with a metal point that created indentations on the discs, letting off a sound.[3] Edison saw that the "accident" had possibly given him a way to record sound permanently. He passed the idea along to his assistants, who set out to produce a working model.

The machine his assistants eventually came up with had a thin membrane that would vibrate when it picked up sound waves, a needle, and a long cylinder covered with metal foil. A crank was attached to turn the cylinder to record the sound. A piece of metal, shaped like the bell-shaped end of a trumpet, was fixed on top to catch the sounds.

When everything was in place, Edison put the machine on a table and turned the crank. As the cylinder revolved, he spoke loudly into the machine:

Mary had a little lamb,
Its fleece was white as snow;
And everywhere that Mary went
The lamb was sure to go.[4]

As Edison was speaking, the needle cut grooves into the foil. When he finished reciting the poem, he returned the needle to the beginning and once again turned the crank. As the cylinder revolved, the needle fit into the grooves and reproduced Edison's voice. Although he had faith that his invention would work, Edison was still somewhat astonished to hear his own voice repeating, "Mary had a little lamb . . ."

In December 1877, Edison registered a patent on his phonograph, and overnight he became a celebrity. Newspaper reporters streamed into Edison's home and laboratory. They began to refer to him as the "Wizard of Menlo Park." More and more visitors came to see and hear his amazing machine.

At Edison's invitation an opera star who sang soprano came to the lab. As Edison turned the cylinder, the woman sang. When she had finished, Edison replayed the song. She was amazed to hear the phonograph repeating her voice exactly. Edison also invited another musician to play a coronet in front of the phonograph. Edison played a trick on the musician by gradually turning the cylinder faster and faster. When replayed, the resulting sound suddenly turned into a hideous shriek. The crowd, who had gathered to hear this new machine, laughed and cheered.

Edison had many other ideas for using the phonograph. It could be used for dictating letters, to create the sounds in music boxes, or as a voice box for a talking doll. In order to make some of these ideas work, Edison set up a company for improving and marketing the phonograph. For a few months, the Edison

A Working Vacation

Edison, a hard worker, rarely took a vacation. Even when he took a trip west with scientists from the University of Pennsylvania, his active brain continued to work. While he was away, he experimented with a device called a tasimeter, which could measure heat. Edison tried to measure the heat changes in the atmosphere during an eclipse, when the moon was blocking the sun's light. Because of problems with bad weather and because the eclipse lasted only about three minutes, Edison was unable to complete his experiment accurately. The experience, however, did give him ideas for further experimentation with the tasimeter, and he eventually considered using it to map the heavens, to locate icebergs from a ship, and to detect body temperature.

Speaking Phonograph Company made money by exhibiting the phonograph. Those who wanted to hear the invention for themselves were charged an entrance fee for the show.

Becoming a Famous Inventor

While the phonograph appealed to ordinary citizens, it also drew attention from the scientific community. Members of the Academy of Science invited Edison to speak at one of their meetings. Edison, whose hearing had continued to deteriorate since his childhood, brought Batch along. Batch would be able to give the talk and answer the questions of the audience better than Edison could do himself, since his hearing was so poor.

In 1878, Edison also received an invitation from President Rutherford B. Hayes to visit the White House and bring along his new invention. Edison brought the phonograph as requested.

The president was fascinated by it and had Edison play the phonograph over and over.[5]

After this burst of publicity, Edison put aside working on improvements on the phonograph. The invention had disappointed Edison somewhat. Though it was an interesting novelty item that drew spectators, Edison thought that at the time of its invention, it really had no practical use. It also did not reproduce sound very well, and very few people were interested in actually owning a phonograph of their own.

The thirty-one-year-old inventor finally admitted that he was tired and needed a change. With a group of scientists, he took a month-long trip through the western states. Although the change of scenery and the conversations with fellow scientists were welcome, Edison was glad when they returned home. It was on this trip that he came up with the idea for the lightbulb, and he was eager to begin the work that would propel him to even greater fame.

Chapter 6

TRAGEDY AND TRIUMPH

Edison's work upon returning home from his western trip resulted in the 1879 invention of the lightbulb. Although this was an exciting event, there was no practical way to make use of the new invention yet. The main problem was that few homes and businesses were wired with the electricity needed to power the lightbulbs. Knowing that he could not immediately begin to market his invention successfully, Edison set to work trying to make the electric light as perfect and practical as possible. He wanted the lightbulb to be of maximum value when he was ready to bring it to homes and offices everywhere.

New Uses for Electricity

Not content to sit back and enjoy his success, with characteristic enthusiasm Edison went to work exploring new ideas that the availability of electricity from power generating stations could make possible. In 1880, on the grounds of Menlo Park, near Christie Street, he laid a short railroad track. Edison built a small electric locomotive, which had a one-hundred-horsepower engine and could travel at speeds of up to forty miles per hour. He created new ways of running and braking a train and did the test runs himself.

Of course, Edison also devoted serious effort to what became his main task after the initial invention of the electric light. He went about trying to improve his lightbulb, while also working on solving the problem of how to bring electricity effectively and cheaply to homes and businesses. Edison continued to perfect the original bulb by using filaments made of bamboo. They burned for a longer amount of time than those made of thread. Edison installed a large number of these new bulbs to light his laboratory. He also considered many different options for providing the electric power needed to run his lighting system to the public.

Edison's Power Plants

Soon he found the answer he was looking for—the construction of electric power plants. Such plants required generators and power cables to deliver electricity to a home or business. Edison and some associates built the Pearl Street Station, an electric power plant, which opened in New York City on September 4, 1882. The plant used six dynamos to generate electric power and send it through insulated, underground lines.

This was the world's first commercially successful central station for the distribution of electricity. The business of providing electricity expanded so rapidly that within a few years, Edison himself was no longer involved with running the power companies. In 1892, several electric companies combined to form a major business, the General Electric Company (GE). By the end of the nineteenth century, there were five hundred Edison plants in the United States that routed electricity to homes and factories. In addition, there were at least fifty of his central stations in foreign countries, including Chile, Italy, Russia, and South Africa. Edison and his work had become world famous.

Death in the Family

In 1884, tragedy struck the Edison family. On April 11, Mary's father, sixty-one-year-old Nicholas Stilwell, died. Mary, already suffering from severe headaches and attacks of nerves, was deeply affected by his death and became seriously ill herself. Edison put aside his work and rushed to his wife's side. In spite of Edison's care, twenty-nine-year-old Mary died on August 9. That morning Marion, who was just twelve years old, found her father in tears by his wife's bedside.[1]

Mary was buried in Newark, New Jersey. Her death was a heavy blow to Edison and the children. Marion, who was very upset, asked why her mother had died. Trying to give his daughter an answer she could understand, Edison said that Mary had died of typhoid fever. (At the time, the disease was widespread in the area.) It was not true, however. Though historians are not certain of the exact cause of Mary's death, they do know that Edison was trying to protect his daughter from knowing that her mother had died after years of fighting a nervous disorder.

Throughout their married life, Mary had been reclusive and timid. She had frequently complained of headaches and sore throats, which doctors felt were physical symptoms of her emotional distress. Mental health science was not as sophisticated then as it is today. When Mary died, her doctors said that the cause of death was a "congestion of the brain," brought on by the strain of living in a rapidly changing urban environment. The doctors believed her "burdened" female brain could not adjust to the constant change of new inventions and new ideas.[2] Because mental illness was not understood as well in the nineteenth century as it is now, there was often a stigma attached to those suffering from nervous disorders. For this reason, Thomas Edison thought that a physical illness would be easier for his daughter, Marion, to accept as a cause of her mother's death than a mental one. It may be possible that Edison lied to his daughter needlessly. Some recent biographers believe that Mary may have had a brain tumor or hemorrhage, which actually caused her death.[3]

Leaving Menlo Park

For a while after Mary passed away, Marion tried to take her mother's place. Edison isolated himself from friends and business acquaintances for over six months. At the same time he tried to do his work, but found it difficult. Eventually, he and the children moved away from Menlo Park. Edison never returned.

In the days after Mary's death, Marion became a source of comfort and a favorite companion for her father. The father and daughter did many things together. Edison, who had spent his youth with working-class people in the telegraph industry, enjoyed popular forms of entertainment that some people at the time may have considered low-class. Marion often accompanied her father to minstrel shows at nightclubs, where the jokes could sometimes be rather crude. Because Edison's hearing was so poor, Marion would tap out the show dialogue in Morse code on her father's hand so he would thoroughly enjoy the performance.

Although he would go out on occasion, especially with Marion, Edison remained grief-stricken and kept to himself for some time. Almost a year after Mary's death, her mother, Margaret Crane Stilwell, thought it would be a good idea for Edison to go away for a while, believing that he needed a change. She offered to care for the Edison children. Edison was grateful and planned a trip with old friends, Ezra Gilliland and his wife, Lillian.

Reunion with an Old Friend

Edison and Ezra Gilliland had met when they both worked as telegraph operators in Adrian, Michigan, and had even been roommates for a while. The two had gone their separate ways until after Edison moved to Newark, New Jersey, and began working on his electric pen in 1874.[4] For a time, Gilliland had worked with Edison on developing the pen, before leaving to take a job running the experimental department of the American Bell Telephone Company in Boston. Shortly after Mary's death, the old friends reunited when Edison's company became involved in a business deal with American Bell. Their friendship was renewed, and Edison decided that Gilliland would be the ideal traveling companion for the trip Mary's mother had suggested.

While on vacation, Edison and the Gillilands visited a World Industrial and Cotton Centennial in New Orleans, Louisiana. At the exhibit Edison saw Lewis Miller from Akron, Ohio, who had previously visited the Menlo Park lab. Miller was accompanied by his nineteen-year-old daughter, Mina. Edison was drawn to Mina's charm and beauty and soon formally asked Miller if he might call on his daughter.

Considering his intelligence and his place in society, some historians have suggested that Edison may have planned to run into the Millers in New Orleans. He may have felt it was time he remarried, and thought Mina, the sophisticated daughter of a wealthy businessman, was someone who could be a suitable new wife for a man of his social and economic position.[5]

A New Wife

After a brief courtship, Edison proposed to the lovely Mina. According to Marion's memoirs, Edison made the proposal by tapping out the question in Morse code on Mina's hand while riding in a carriage.[6] Whether he used Morse code or not, Edison got his point across. Mina agreed to marry him. On February 24, 1886, she married Edison in a large wedding ceremony at her parents' home.[7]

Edison's new wife was petite with olive skin and brown eyes, the seventh child in a family of eleven. She had many social skills as well as a large group of friends. When Edison first began seeing her, Mina was already engaged to a minister's son. Although her fiancé came from a respectable family, Mina's father was always conscious of money matters, and felt that a better match could be made for his daughter.

When Edison asked for Miller's permission to marry Mina, Miller more than happily agreed. In Miller's eyes, the match made sense. Edison was rich and famous, able to provide for Mina's needs, while Mina was a sophisticated young woman with a wide knowledge of social affairs. Mina's social contacts and skill at entertaining influential people could be of benefit to Edison, who still sometimes tended to be reclusive as he tried to work on his inventions. Both Edison and Mina were imaginative, creative people who were used to being involved in different aspects of business, commerce, and socializing. Together they could make a good team.[8]

While Edison took his new bride on a two-month honeymoon trip to Fort Myers, Florida, Margaret Stilwell again looked after her grandchildren. At that time, Fort Myers was a quiet place where many kinds of tropical plants and trees grew. Edison, who had first heard about the town from a railroad station manager while traveling with the Gillilands, thought it was an ideal place for winter vacations. It would be a perfect location to get away from the cold, wet weather of the northern winters. Edison decided to build a home in the area.

Retreat at Fort Myers

His friend Gilliland also found the area pleasant. Gilliland and Edison established a joint account of $27,000 to be used to construct buildings in the area, with houses near each other and a laboratory for Edison. The two homes were connected by a pathway so that the Edison and Gilliland families could easily visit back and forth.[9]

The prefabricated walls, shipped from Maine, were among the first of their kind to be used in the South. While construction of the "twin" houses was underway, Edison also supervised work on a Fort Myers laboratory that would be similar to the early one in Menlo Park.

A New Home at Glenmont

Meanwhile, Edison was preparing a surprise for his new wife. He had purchased Glenmont, a large Victorian home in Llewellyn Park, a residential area of West Orange, New Jersey. Llewellyn Park was the first planned residential suburb in the United States. Although Edison might have preferred to live in New York City, where most of his friends and the other top inventors and businessmen of the day were living, Mina liked the area of Llewellyn Park. It was to please her that Edison had purchased the house and was having it cleaned and prepared for them. The home, originally red, was a brick and clapboard building with many gables and balconies, and twenty-nine rooms. Standing on thirteen acres, Glenmont cost nearly a quarter of a million dollars. Aside from the building itself and the grounds, with well-maintained gardens, all the furnishings—sofas, tables, chairs, beds, and a library filled with shelves of books—were included in the purchase price.[10] When the couple returned from Florida, Mina was delighted with her new home.

Enjoying Family Life

The three children from Edison's first marriage rarely spent time at Glenmont, since they attended boarding schools. When they did come home, however, Edison would sometimes play games like Parcheesi and billiards with the children. School vacations were especially carefree. The favorite family celebration was the

Fourth of July, when Edison would arrange a huge fireworks and rocket display at Glenmont home.

After settling into their new home, the Edisons went on with their lives. Young Mina Edison entertained guests in the parlor while her husband made plans to build a new laboratory just down the hill from Glenmont. This new lab in West Orange would be ten times larger than the one at Menlo Park. Happy with his surroundings and his new wife, Edison was ready to go to work again.

Busy Workdays

For the rest of his life, the West Orange lab near Glenmont would be like a second home to Edison. When he arrived each morning, he looked through his mail. Then, for the next hour, his employees conferred with him on the day's projects. At any given time there were usually between forty-five and sixty employees working in the lab, though at times the number of workers rose as high as two hundred. After the morning conference, the day's work began. Often when there was an exciting experiment being conducted, Edison and his employees worked long past dark.

Like the Menlo Park lab, Edison's West Orange laboratory was to be devoted completely to working on experiments, rather than to making and selling products. The lab contained a two-story library, filled with thousands of reference books. Edison and his workers could go there to get information for carrying out their experiments.

The new West Orange laboratory would, like its Menlo Park predecessor, eventually become the setting for many important inventions. Shortly after setting up the West Orange lab in 1888–1889, Edison and one of his trusted assistants, W. K. L. Dickson, began experimenting with celluloid film. They found a way to record a series of images—each showing a tiny move forward. If the subject was a baseball player, for example, his bat would be on his shoulder in the first image, held wide in the next, moving toward the ball in the next, and finally connecting with the ball for a hit. When the images were viewed in rapid succession, they would give the impression of real movement.

The Kinetoscope

For the next five years, Edison and his assistants worked on an invention called the kinetoscope. The filmstrip system was enclosed in a machine with a viewing device. A person put a coin in a slot, looked into the viewer, and turned a handle. The faster the handle turned, the faster the images of the actors on the film moved. This invention led to an even more interesting one. By 1888, regarding his initial work on the kinetoscope, Edison reported that he was now "experimenting upon an instrument which does for the Eye what the phonograph does for the Ear."[11]

In 1893, Dickson, under Edison's direction, built a huge, ugly building at the West Orange lab. The building, covered with black tar paper, was called the "Black Maria." It looked like a police paddy wagon, used to carry prisoners, which was often called a "Black Maria." The black siding helped keep the interior dark enough for camera work. A section of the building's black roof could be opened to admit enough light for a successful "shoot," and the building, mounted on a large pivot, could be rotated to catch the light.[12]

The First Movie Studio

Beginning in 1894, in this place, with his strange, ugly building representing what would become the world's first movie studio, Thomas Edison laid the foundation for the motion-picture industry. Favorite subjects for early motion pictures included boxing matches, circus acts, and animals. Not all of the films were

The Kinetoscope

The name for Edison's famous invention comes from the Greek word kinesis, which means "motion." Edison was able to find a simple way to make a filmstrip revolve by perforating its edges and passing it over sprockets. An electric motor kept the sprockets turning, so that the filmstrip, and the images on it, could move constantly.

The Columbian Exposition

Thomas Alva Edison presented his first commercial motion-picture machine, the kinetoscope, at the World's Columbian Exposition of 1893. Held in Chicago, the exposition was a gigantic fair that celebrated the four hundredth anniversary of Christopher Columbus's discovery of the New World.

very exciting. One of the earliest films actually featured one of Edison's employees sneezing![13]

Over the years, Edison and his company would continue to improve the kinetoscope, making films for individual viewers and adding sound to accompany the moving pictures. Eventually, other companies would also make improvements in the technology, thus advancing the early motion-picture industry.

In addition to motion pictures, Edison continued to work on other new ideas and to have a great deal of success. By the early years of the twentieth century, his West Orange lab had produced an improved phonograph machine with a larger sound receiver, disc records with revolving plates that stored sound, several dictating machines, the motion-picture camera, the kinetoscope, an improved storage battery, and a magnetic method for extracting and separating low-grade iron ore from pure samples.

Edison's "invention factory" had succeeded not only in bringing Edison's ideas to the attention of the whole world, but also in making Edison himself a very wealthy man. By the end of the nineteenth century, Thomas Edison, who had started off life as the son of a modest businessman in the Midwest and had worked long hours at hard and sometimes menial jobs, owned combined assets valued at more than $10 million. He was becoming rich in many different ways.

Chapter 7

EXPLORING
NEW IDEAS

In addition to the three children from Edison's first marriage, Thomas and Mina Edison had three children of their own— Madeleine in 1888, Charles in 1890, and Theodore in 1898. Glenmont was a busy household, with the activities of the three youngest Edison children and frequent visits by the other children and many family friends. Unlike Thomas Edison's first wife, Mary, Mina was accustomed to the company of well-known and influential people and greatly enjoyed entertaining both friends and the famous people who called on her husband. Among their visitors over the years were Orville Wright, one of the inventors of the airplane, and Guglielmo Marconi, the famous Italian physicist who developed the wireless radio.

Edison's closest friends were usually business associates, who had the most in common with him. But his ready sense of humor and intelligent conversation drew many other people to him, both young and old. Edison was a favorite subject of interviews with journalists because of his friendly, cooperative, and casual personality.

New Factory at Schenectady

In 1886, Edison learned that an abandoned factory in Schenectady, New York, was for sale. He bought it for forty-five thousand dollars and moved his city machine works to this new location. As usual, Edison was right beside his workers—planning, advising, and encouraging them. When he was satisfied that the factory was running smoothly, he put John Kruesi in charge of the two hundred factory employees.[1]

It was a four-hour train ride from Glenmont in West Orange to the new factory in Schenectady. Even in cold weather Edison made regular visits. While there, he often walked back and forth between the yard and the building. Some historians believe that the stress of constantly changing his work environment and plans finally began to take its toll. Before long, he became very ill. Edison left for the warm climate of Fort Myers, where it took him three months to recover.

Trying the Iron Ore Business

By 1890, Edison and his associates owned and operated several companies. Edison became as talented a businessman as he was a scientist and inventor. Most of his businesses were doing well. When he heard of a failing business in northern New Jersey, Edison decided to try to revive it. Because the venture was risky, he planned to finance it alone. He bought twenty-five hundred acres of land near Ogdensburg, New Jersey, where a surface mine had been operating since the late 1700s. Edison re-created the entire area. He designed huge equipment and set up a very impressive plant to remove the raw iron ore and process it to make it usable in his different businesses.

An oversized, mechanical steam shovel dug up the iron ore. Then, in the plant, equipment separated the low-grade ore from the tailings, or residue. The best ore was shipped to steel manufacturing plants, mostly in Pennsylvania. It was a huge undertaking. For a period of five years, Edison spent most of his time at the site. From Tuesday through Friday, he was at the plant. On Saturday, he returned to his West Orange laboratory to catch up on its current work. Then, he spent Sunday with his family at Glenmont, and he traveled back to the Ogdensburg plant on Monday.

Difficult Times at Home

Over the years that he worked with the Ogdensburg mine, Edison and his family suffered the pains of frequent separations. His daughter, Madeleine, later recalled seeing her father as little more than an unfamiliar "presence" during those years.[2] The Edisons' marriage also showed signs of strain.

As had happened in his first marriage, Edison tended to regard his work as the most important aspect of his life, something that could not be carried on without his personal direction. This led to frequent absences from home, especially during the years of operation of the Ogdensburg mine, and Mina became increasingly unhappy. Historians have found letters Edison wrote to Mina during this time, trying to convince her to visit him at the mine site. Mina's letters to Edison have not been located, but many believe that Mina was somewhat resentful of Edison's absence and, being accustomed to luxury, she was probably reluctant to stay in the uncomfortable surroundings in which Edison lived while at the mine.[3]

In spite of Edison's remarkable work at the mine, the plant began to run at a financial loss. This had nothing to do with Edison's techniques, but rather with his competition. A large deposit of iron ore had been discovered in Minnesota. That ore was near the surface and was of a higher grade, which made it better than the ore being provided by Edison's mine. Edison finally closed his mining operation in 1901.

Henry Ford

In 1896, Edison met Henry Ford, a young man who was also interested in inventions, at a company dinner in New York City. Sixteen years younger than Thomas Edison, Ford admired the older man. Edison encouraged Ford to keep working toward his goal—building a car that would be inexpensive enough for almost anyone in the United States to afford.

Although the two would not meet again for sixteen years after their introduction in New York, this meeting set the tone for what would later become a long friendship. In spite of their age difference, Henry Ford and Thomas Edison became very close friends, most likely because they had so much in common. Both men were successful businessmen who had devoted their lives to coming up with new ideas that would make life easier for people all over the world. Their similar goals and careers made for an affectionate and respectful friendship that would last for the rest of Edison's life. As a token of that friendship, every year at Christmas, Edison found a gift from Henry Ford—a brand new Ford automobile—parked in his driveway.

Five Wizards in the Wild

In 1916, the two friends began to take annual camping trips together. They were joined by other men who were achieving fame and fortune in the American business and science communities. Among them were Harvey Firestone, a rubber manufacturer; John Burroughs, a naturalist, who enjoyed studying plants and animals; and R. J. H. De Loach, a college professor. The group became popularly known as the "Five Wizards in the Wild." Despite the wilderness implied in the nickname, however, they brought many of the comforts of home with them on their camping trips.

In fact, preparations for each trip were quite elaborate. The group traveled to the campsite in at least three elegant touring cars, including Firestone's Packard, taking along four or five trucks loaded with food and camping equipment, as well as several servants. Edison often commented that they looked like a traveling circus group with all their unusual camping gear. Once they reached their campsite, the servants erected the tents, built fires, and served food to the "Wizards." It was a special time for relaxing, reading, and exchanging ideas.[4]

Life at Home

When Edison was not enjoying the company of his friends in science and business, he found many different ways to enjoy himself. Mina continued to make sure that daily life in the Edison home ran smoothly. She also did a great deal of entertaining, hosting simple get-togethers for friends, family, and the many dignitaries who often came to see Edison. Over the years, however, there were times when she went to great lengths to make her family feel special. On Madeleine's thirteenth birthday in 1901, for example, Mina invited forty children to Glenmont for an elaborate party. The guests played games in the parlor and outside on the lawn. The grand finale included a huge birthday cake decorated with small American flags. The following month, Theodore turned three years old. Mina made sure he got to celebrate in his own way, getting him a large cake that was shaped like a locomotive.

Making Cement

In the year 1900, one of Edison's companies began to produce "Portland" cement, a gray powder used to make concrete. Edison received a patent for his new, more efficient method of producing cement. Eventually, Edison built one of the largest cement plants in the United States. In his new factory Edison put to work much of the technology he had developed for his ore milling project in the 1890s. His cement was used in the construction of roads and buildings. Edison also tried other interesting ways to use the cement. As an experiment he built sturdy concrete furniture for gardens and even for home use. Another notable use of Edison's cement was at Yankee Stadium, a famous New York baseball park. Over 180,000 bags of cement—each bag weighing in at ninety-four pounds—were poured into its foundation.

Edison's skills, however, were not only used to produce inventions that would make life more interesting and fun. He also tried to serve his country by providing advice on projects that concerned the safety and well-being of the United States and the whole world.

World War I

In 1914, World War I broke out in Europe. Officially neutral, Americans at first watched the developing crisis from a distance. Then, an English passenger ship, the *Lusitania*, was hit by a German torpedo and sank. About twelve hundred people drowned, including more than one hundred Americans. The attack alarmed the United States government and its people, and by 1917, the United States had formally entered the war on the side of the Allies against Germany and the Central Powers.

Serving His Country

World War I changed the lives of Americans everywhere. It also drastically changed the business of Thomas Edison. In 1915, the United States Congress decided to start a special research laboratory for the Navy, the Naval Consulting Board. Its job was to find ways to better protect United States ships from German underwater attacks. As early as 1895, when he first sensed the problems brewing in international politics, Edison had declared that he would drop everything in order to serve his country in whatever way he could if a war did come. So when the United States entered World War I, Edison was a natural choice to chair the new Naval Consulting Board. Edison was invited to Washington, D.C., to participate in the project. For eighteen months, he worked in the government lab, which was designed to resemble closely the lab he had left back home in West Orange. While there, he perfected several items for use against submarine attacks.[5]

The period during the war was especially difficult because Edison's companies were converted from producing mostly commercial goods to making wartime materials. Luckily, because of Edison's habit of always keeping up with the trends of current affairs, the West Orange lab was prepared for just such a conversion, even before America entered the war in Europe.

When Edison joined the Naval Consulting Board in 1915, his son Charles stepped in to manage business affairs in West Orange and to make sure everything was done efficiently in his father's absence.[6] Although a little fearful because of the national attention earned by his famous father, Charles was a good worker and was able to handle the responsibilities well. When Edison returned, he found the books and the businesses in good order.

Charles Edison would later earn national fame in his own right. He was eventually elected governor of New Jersey, and also served in President Franklin Roosevelt's Cabinet as assistant secretary and then secretary of the Navy. He would carry on the legacy of his famous father in arenas that Edison himself had never considered, such as politics.

The End of the War

The war ended with Germany's defeat in 1918. It had been the most bloody and devastating war in world history to that time, and it had brought with it many changes that would affect people

Treaty of Versailles

Signed on June 28, 1919, the Treaty of Versailles officially ended World War I. Among its provisions, the treaty forced Germany to accept the blame for the war and made the defeated Central Powers repay the victorious Allies as punishment for starting the war. The treaty also led to the formation of the League of Nations, an organization designed to encourage the countries of the world to meet and talk about their problems in order to avoid future wars.

all over the world. Almost a whole generation of young men had been killed or wounded. In addition, the fighting had embroiled all of the major world powers and had cost huge sums of money. It would be years before the countries involved, especially those that were defeated, would be able to pay off all their debts. However, World War I also brought the United States to a new position of prominence as the richest nation on earth.

The war had also meant new things for Thomas Edison. Because of the success of his companies in contributing to the war effort and his own assistance at the government lab, people began to take serious notice for the first time of Edison's system for inventing. His participation in searching for better ways to fight wars through science had showed the world that research, done in laboratories built exclusively for the purpose of coming up with new ideas and making them work, was an extremely effective technique. After the war was over, Edison and his laboratory would go on to become a model for how corporations and the government would do their research in later years.

Thomas Edison, however, was not content to just rest and enjoy his ever-growing fame. He still had work to do. After he returned from working in Washington, D.C., he went back home to Glenmont to get on with his inventing and his life.

Chapter 8

BECOMING A
LEGEND

Ⓘn the winter of 1925, Edison became ill again. It was becoming customary for him to travel south to a warmer climate when the snow began to fall and ice formed in New Jersey. Mina and Edison once again left for their winter home in Fort Myers, Florida. He gained strength during the mild days and began to think of work again.

Traveling South for the Winter

At that time, Fort Myers was a village on the Caloosahatchee River. There was no bridge from the mainland across the river. The Edisons boarded the electric boat *Reliance*, which took them up the river past hundreds of bamboo plants along its banks. The boat also regularly brought supplies to the town.[1]

During their first visit to Fort Myers in 1886, the Edisons spent time with the Gillilands, enjoying their "twin" homes. However, fourteen years passed before the Edisons returned to stay at Fort Myers, and the Gillilands never returned.[2] When

Gilliland cheated Edison in a business transaction in 1888, their friendship came to an abrupt end. Gilliland had been helping Edison prepare to market his phonograph, but was lured into a deal with one of Edison's competitors. Edison was outraged and tried for years to sue Gilliland and his new business partners for fraud.[3]

After the split with the Gillilands, the Edisons bought the Gilliland home in Fort Myers and decided to combine both of the "twin" houses into one huge complex.[4] The fourteen-foot roofed verandas around the homes protected the Edisons from the Florida rains. The walls of the lower floors were made of glass doors and could be opened to catch the warm breezes.

As a gift for Mina, Edison built a fish pond with lilies, Egyptian papyrus and bulrushes planted all around it. Edison liked to sit at the end of the pier and fish. Most of the time he did not bother to put bait on his hook. He just liked the pier because it gave him a peaceful place to think.

Improving the Area

Always observant and ready to come up with new ideas, Edison turned his attention to nearby roads. The original way onto the Edisons' Fort Myers property was a cattle path through swampy ground. Knowing how inconvenient this was, Edison had a smooth road constructed for miles over the original trail. He imported hundreds of royal palm trees from Cuba and had them planted for a two-mile stretch along the road.[5] The city's officials liked the look of Edison's palm-shaded lane and later extended the palms for several more miles along the road.

An Unusual Garden

When the days were mild, Edison spent much of his time gardening rather than working in the lab. He applied his usual determined effort to gardening. Eventually, he had over six thousand plants and trees planted according to his very specific directions. Some were poisonous, others exotic, but all of them were very interesting. There was a "sausage" tree, with strange growths that resembled sausages, and a tree with buds that looked like an ear. There was a "dynamite" tree, whose fruit was the size of a tomato and literally exploded, scattering seeds up to two hundred feet away. The tree's poisonous sap was believed to have medicinal properties and was sometimes extracted for use in treating spinal meningitis and infantile paralysis.

Edison's gardens also included a "chamois" tree, which had leaves that felt like cloth, and a kapok tree, which provided buoyant material used for life preservers. There were many citrus trees, including one that bore huge lemons, and several spice plants. Bee hives, imported from Holland, supplied honey and helped pollinate the gardens. Edison also grew grapes, pineapple plants, tobacco plants, sugarcane, and more than a thousand varieties of flowers.

Near the house was a swimming pool. Its walls were made of concrete and were reinforced with wild bamboo shoots. Typical of Edison's desire to make one product do the work of two, the pool's remarkable underground water system also watered the huge gardens.

Special Guests

Over the years, many friends of the Edisons came to visit the Fort Myers retreat. Mina frequently asked their famous guests to buy a stepping-stone, have their names carved on it, and return it to her. These were laid along her special "Friendship Walk." When she asked Henry Ford, then a millionaire, to add a stone to the walk, he replied jokingly that he could not afford to pay for the carving of his name. A blank stone was added to the walk for him.

Not only was Henry Ford one of Edison's greatest admirers, he also became a neighbor. Near the Edison home, Ford bought three acres of land and built a handsome fourteen-room winter home for his family. Ford named the huge house, which was completely electrified, The Mangoes. Ford put a gate in the fence between the two homes, so that he could easily visit the Edisons.[6]

Ford and Mina often organized Sunday trips around the town. The Edisons and Fords dressed in their finest holiday clothes, and John Scarth, Edison's chauffeur, drove them along the streets of Fort Myers and into the surrounding countryside. Those Sundays, during their special drives, were the only times that Edison would dress formally in a suit and white shirt with a high starched collar. Most of the time he still preferred simple clothing that would not be ruined by his dirty work in the laboratory and that was comfortable enough for him to work in.

Fort Myers offered lots of opportunities for the Edisons. In addition to hosting many visitors, Mina became a member of the local Audubon Society, a group for people interested in birds and bird-watching. She also joined the local garden club and frequently played golf with other Fort Myers ladies. When she could persuade Edison to put aside his work, Mina sometimes drove the two of them to the Arcade Theater in Fort Myers. Because Edison's hearing was so bad, Mina would tap out the movie dialogue in Morse code on the back of her husband's hand, just as Marion had done at minstrel shows many years earlier.

New Business Ideas

Fort Myers also gave Edison interesting new ideas for business. His early days as a telegrapher had given him the opportunity to learn current news and helped him develop a broad knowledge of politics and business around the country. He had kept up with the news throughout his life and was always searching for ways to improve the situation he saw around him.

When World War I began, for example, shipments of rubber from Africa and Asia to the United States were stopped by blockades. Edison had many friends in the automobile industry and realized that they needed rubber for tires, belts, and other equipment. He wanted to find a way to keep wars from putting a stop to business. He decided to try to find a plant source for rubber in the United States. His search began in Fort Myers and continued around the country. Edison, as usual, was unwilling to rest until he found what he was looking for.

Edison formed the Edison Botanic Research Corporation to conduct research on developing rubber from American plants.[7] He started the research in his own Fort Myers gardens, with its huge supply of unusual plants. He also visited botanical gardens in New York and at Rutgers University in New Jersey, and went to work to set up his very own center for cultivating herbs and plants in West Orange, where he could conduct further experiments.

Edison meticulously cataloged each plant material that he and his helpers collected for the experiment. After many trials he narrowed his search to the goldenrod plant, a member of the sunflower family, which could be made into usable rubber. Then he began to cultivate the plant.[8] Eventually, Edison's corporation, supervised by his brother-in-law John Miller, succeeded in making each acre of goldenrod yield one hundred pounds of rubber.

The extraction process was complicated. First, the goldenrod plants were hung until thoroughly dried. Then, they were crushed and ground before being put into a still and whirled around. The final step was a drying process. The workers frequently sneezed and coughed as they handled the dry, dusty materials. Edison nicknamed the rubber workshop the Hay Fever Room.[9] Edison's development was a great success. He had found a way to make rubber at home when war or some other problem prevented imported rubber from reaching American businesses.

News of Edison's rubber caused great excitement in the scientific and business communities. Though proud of his work, Edison consistently reminded people that he had "discovered" rather than "invented" this product. The rubber had always been available from the goldenrod plant. He had just found a way to use what was already there. However Edison had come up with it, the product was a great achievement. To celebrate the accomplishment, Harvey Firestone, a tire manufacturer and one of the "Wizards in the Wild," presented Edison with four tires made from the rubber. Although the knowledge that rubber could be manufactured to serve Americans in the event of an emergency was useful, the goldenrod plant never actually produced enough rubber to become competitive with other sources of rubber. So Edison was never able to produce the rubber for real profits.

Different Products

Each spring, when the weather grew warmer, the Edisons returned to New Jersey, where Edison's most important scientific work was usually done. Aside from his major contributions to the world of science and technology, Edison also spent time on a more modest project for children. He opened a small factory, using the leftover space of one of his businesses in Wisconsin, which mostly manufactured children's furniture. The chairs and tables were just the right size for younger people.

A Special Anniversary

In 1928, Henry Ford realized that the year 1929 would mark the fiftieth anniversary of Edison's invention of the lightbulb. In Dearborn, Michigan, Ford began to build an elaborate park filled

Harvey Firestone

Harvey Firestone, one of the "Wizards in the Wild," was an industrialist and a pioneer in the field of automobile tires. He grew up on a farm in Ohio and became interested in rubber tires when he was working for a carriage factory. He founded the Firestone Tire and Rubber Company in Akron, Ohio, in 1900. He served as chairman of the board until his death in 1938.

with reconstructions and restorations of famous buildings in American history. One of these was Edison's Menlo Park laboratory. Edison, Mina, and other guests, including President Herbert Hoover, traveled by train to Dearborn. After a big formal dinner, Ford led Edison to the laboratory, where Edison reenacted the birth of the lightbulb. When he connected two wires, the dark laboratory blazed with light. It was a special night for Edison and his family.[10]

Henry Ford was not alone in his admiration of Edison. By this time, Edison was probably more famous as an inventor than anyone else in the world. Edison had even received the Congressional Medal of Honor in 1928, presented by Andrew W. Mellon, the United States secretary of the treasury.

Honoring the Inventor

In August 1930, President Hoover extended an invitation to Edison to visit the White House. Unfortunately, the inventor was too ill to accept. As winter approached, the Edisons once again went south to Fort Myers for its pleasant climate. Edison, who was becoming more and more frail, spent most of his time there sitting in the sun. He kept himself bundled up in a heavy coat and wrapped in blankets. By the time Edison returned home to New Jersey in June, the inventor was seriously ill.

He became weaker each day. Knowing that Edison's illness was life-threatening and that he would probably not survive much longer, Mina sent for all the Edison children. In October, Edison slipped into a coma. Edison briefly regained consciousness only once. He opened his eyes and told Mina, "It is very beautiful over there."[11] Edison died the next day, on October 18, 1931, at the age of eighty-four.

For two days and nights, his body lay in state in the library of his laboratory at West Orange. A funeral service was held at Glenmont, and then the mourners followed Edison's casket to

The Congressional Medal of Honor

The highest honor given in the United States, the Congressional Medal of Honor was first awarded in 1863. Although normally reserved for those who perform extraordinary military feats, it has been bestowed upon a select few civilians for their contributions to the country. In 1928, President Calvin Coolidge honored Edison with the award for the practical and imaginative talent he had used to help make life easier for the people of the United States.

nearby Rosedale Cemetery. After final prayers each mourner left a white rose at Edison's grave.

On the evening of Edison's funeral, President Hoover gave a special radio address to the public. He asked citizens across the country to turn down the lights in their homes and businesses as a tribute to the man who had given them the lightbulb. Even the Statue of Liberty's torch was dimmed in honor of Edison.

From his earliest days, Edison had been ambitious and optimistic. He did not concentrate on just the present, but always looked ahead. He designed a unique laboratory and employed a specially trained team of workers for one single purpose: inventions. Many people considered him a genius.

Edison's own words best describe his lifelong belief: "Genius is 1 percent inspiration and 99 percent perspiration." Of course, his talents and scientific abilities were enormous, but Edison himself made it clear that talent and ambition are not enough to achieve success. He always attributed his own brilliant career as an inventor to hard work and determination.

Chapter 9

AN EXCEPTIONAL LEGACY

Edison's one-hundred-fiftieth birthday was celebrated in 1997. In honor of the event, the staff at the Edison National Historic Site in West Orange, New Jersey, planned a tribute to Edison's life and work. This celebration was one way in which Edison was remembered. In 1979, historians at the Edison National Historic Site began the enormous task of collecting Edison's papers and scientific notes. Called the Papers Project, it included the tedious work of going through drawers, cabinets, and files at the site. At the end, nearly 5 million documents had been gathered together. They estimated there was enough material to fill twenty volumes and take as much as ten years to have those materials cataloged and ready for publication.

Remembering Thomas Edison

There are several major sites and museums in different states devoted to Thomas Edison. Throughout his long life, Edison had an impact on a great many people and places. Among the sites that celebrate Edison and his contributions to science are the restored brick home in Milan, Ohio, where Edison was born; the winter homes, pool, and gardens in Fort Myers, Florida; and a restored Menlo Park laboratory, which was moved to Dearborn, Michigan, by Edison's longtime friend, Henry Ford. There is also a memorial tower devoted to Edison on the site of his first innovative laboratory in Menlo Park, New Jersey.

All of these memorials attempt to record the activities and inventions of a most remarkable man. Edison created a research and manufacturing complex, the first of its kind in the world. He filled his laboratory with talented engineers and scientists. His research lab became the model for today's complex centers for corporate research and development.

Overcoming Obstacles

What is perhaps most unique about the life of Thomas Edison is how he overcame great difficulties to achieve all that he did. He frequently told his lab workers that he had not been able to hear a bird's song since he was twelve years old. Such a loss of hearing over the years might have prevented many people from striving for their goals. But Edison was different. With characteristic humor and a positive attitude, he pointed out that his increasing deafness made it far easier to concentrate on a difficult project. Because he could not hear the grinding of machinery and the blast of a lab furnace, he was able to concentrate with a great intensity on whatever project was at hand. In his quiet world, Edison produced many amazing inventions. He proved overwhelmingly that a handicap need not be the end of a productive life.

Throughout history, there has never been another man quite like Edison, and most likely there never will be one. With his cheerfulness, optimism, drive, sense of humor, and ability, he instilled confidence in his workers. As a man who had spent years working late shifts in dirty offices as a telegraph operator, Edison never lost his sense of being an ordinary worker. Unlike many other employers, Edison worked side by side with his employees, and tried to be just like any one of them, despite the fact that his personal abilities automatically made him stand out from the crowd. His remarkable patience and down-to-earth style constantly inspired those who worked with him to keep searching for the answer to whatever problem they were trying to solve. Always confident in what could be accomplished through hard work, Edison was convinced that the solution to a problem or a new invention was right around the corner. And it usually was.

Examples of his unfailing determination can be found in his search for just the right filament for the lightbulb and the hundreds of plants he tested in his quest to find a domestic source for rubber. Though the tasks proved difficult, Edison never allowed himself to give up. He searched everywhere and anywhere to find the right tools and the right products. He did not stop until he discovered what he was looking for. He was fond of saying that to be a successful inventor, a person would need imagination and a good scrap heap. He understood that inventing products that would make everyday life easier for

Edison Memorial Tower

The memorial tower in Menlo Park, New Jersey—the site of Edison's first laboratory dedicated exclusively to producing inventions—was built to commemorate Edison's ninety-first birthday. The gigantic "bulb" at its top uses 5,200 watts of electricity.

people often involved difficult, tedious, and sometimes dirty work. When Edison first visited the reconstruction of his lab in Michigan, he remarked to Henry Ford that in the original building in Menlo Park, the floors were never so clean.

A Legacy of Inventions

With the help of his faithful lab workers, Edison was able to create many inventions that were early versions of numerous products still in use, and to develop improvements in many other products. In addition to motion pictures, the phonograph and records, the electric lightbulb and the power system that made it glow, and the electric railroad, Edison's work led to the manufacture of many other household items. Edison was the one who showed how electricity could be brought into individual homes and businesses, which would later allow families to use such inventions as electric blenders, fans, refrigerators, ranges, and coffee percolators. Edison's inventions are also the forerunners of the television, videocassette recorder, and compact disc player.

Over the years, Edison received 1,093 patents on products that he invented or improved. No other inventor before or since has recorded so many inventions, discoveries, or improvements on existing products. Daring, persevering, and productive, Thomas Alva Edison set up the world's first research laboratory, now considered essential for industry. His work was a gift to science and to people everywhere that continues to make lives better today.

CHRONOLOGY

1847—Born in Milan, Ohio.

1854—Edison family moves to Port Huron, Michigan.

1859—Begins work on the Grand Trunk Railroad.

1862—Learns basics of telegraphy; Begins work as a telegraph operator.

1868—Moves to the main Western Union telegraph office in Boston; Applies for his first patent.

1869—Issued his first patent; Moves to New York City.

1870—Establishes his first manufacturing shop in Newark, New Jersey.

1871—Marries Mary Stilwell.

1874—Designs the quadruplex telegraph.

1876—Builds famous laboratory in Menlo Park, New Jersey.

1877—Invents the phonograph; Improves the telephone.

1879—Invents the lightbulb.

1882—Builds a New York electric power plant at Pearl Street.

1884—Wife, Mary, dies.

1886—Marries Mina Miller; Moves to Llewellyn Park, a suburb of West Orange, New Jersey.

1887—Builds huge lab in West Orange, New Jersey; Builds lab in Fort Myers, Florida.

1888—Begins experiments on motion pictures; Begins work on developing a commercial model of the phonograph; Invents the kinetoscope.

1894—Builds experimental movie studio.

1900—Begins building large Portland cement plant in New Jersey.

1915—Serves on United States Naval Consulting Board during World War I.

1928—Awarded Congressional Medal of Honor.

1931—Dies at his home in Llewellyn Park.

CHAPTER NOTES

Chapter 1. The Birth of Electric Light

1. Neil Baldwin, *Edison: Inventing the Century* (New York: Hyperion, 1995), p. 104.

2. Matthew Josephson, *Edison: A Biography*, rev. ed. (New York: John Wiley, 1992), p. 220.

3. Baldwin, p. 111.

4. Ibid., p. 113.

5. Robert Silverberg, *Light for the World* (Princeton, N.J.: Van Nostrand, 1967), pp. 136–138.

Chapter 2. An Ambitious Childhood

1. Reese V. Jenkins et al., eds., *The Papers of Thomas Edison* (Baltimore: Johns Hopkins University Press, 1989), vol. 1, pp. 3–6.

2. Ibid.

3. Neil Baldwin, Edison: *Inventing the Century* (New York: Hyperion, 1995), p. 17.

4. Idrisyn Oliver Evans, *Inventors of the World* (New York: Frederick Warne, 1962), p. 105.

5. Baldwin, p. 18.

6. Nina Morgan, *Thomas Edison* (New York: Bookwright Press, 1991), p. 7.

7. Baldwin, p. 22.

8. Ibid., pp. 24–25.

9. Ibid., p. 26.

10. Morgan, p. 8.

11. David A. Adler, *Thomas Alva Edison: Great Inventor* (New York: Holiday House, 1990), p. 17.

12. Enid La Monte Meadowcroft, *The Story of Thomas Alva Edison* New York: Grosset & Dunlop, 1952), pp. 6–13.

13. Matthew Josephson, *Edison: A Biography*, rev. ed. (New York: John Wiley, 1992), p. 36.

14. Baldwin, p. 32.

15. Ibid.

16. Ibid., p. 36.

Chapter 3. The Young Telegrapher

1. Robert Conot, *A Streak of Luck* (New York: Seaview Books, 1979), pp. 21–22.

2. Ibid., pp. 22–23.

3. Ibid., pp. 23–24.

4. Neil Baldwin, *Edison: Inventing the Century* (New York: Hyperion, 1995), p. 42.

5. Ibid., p. 47.

Chapter 4. Starting a Career as an Inventor

1. Robert Conot, *A Streak of Luck* (New York: Seaview Books, 1979), p. 33.

2. Neil Baldwin, *Edison: Inventing the Century* (New York: Hyperion, 1995), p. 50.

3. Matthew Josephson, *Edison: A Biography*, rev. ed. (New York: John Wiley, 1992), p. 87.

4. Andre Millard, *Edison and the Business of Innovation* (Baltimore: Johns Hopkins University Press, 1990), p. 33.

5. Conot, p. 47.

6. Baldwin, p. 67.

7. Ibid., pp. 60–61.

8. Ibid., p. 67.

Chapter 5. The Invention Factory at Menlo Park

1. Neil Baldwin, *Edison: Inventing the Century* (New York: Hyperion, 1995), pp. 68–69.

2. Matthew Josephson, *Edison: A Biography*, rev. ed. (New York: John Wiley, 1992), p. 134.

3. Francis Jehl, *Menlo Park Reminiscences* (Dearborn, Mich.: Edison Institute, 1937), vol. 1, p. 162.

4. Baldwin, p. 82.

5. David Adler, *Thomas Alva Edison: Great Inventor* (New York: Holiday House, 1990), p. 37.

Chapter 6. Tragedy and Triumph

1. Neil Baldwin, *Edison: Inventing the Century* (New York: Hyperion, 1995), p. 143.

2. Ibid., pp. 134, 143.

3. Robert Silverberg, *Light for the World* (Princeton, N.J.: Van Nostrand, 1967), p. 61.

4. Baldwin, p. 147.

5. Ibid., p. 159.

6. David Adler, *Thomas Alva Edison: Great Inventor* (New York: Holiday House, 1990), p. 44.

7. Baldwin, p. 161.

8. Robert Conot, *A Streak of Luck* (New York: Seaview Books, 1979), pp. 239–240.

9. Baldwin, p. 167.

10. Ibid., p. 211.

11. Conot, p. 327.

12. Baldwin, p. 239.

13. Ibid.

Chapter 7. Exploring New Ideas

1. Neil Baldwin, *Edison: Inventing the Century* (New York: Hyperion, 1995), p. 178.

2. Ibid., p. 247.

3. Ibid., p. 248.

4. Robert Conot, *A Streak of Luck* (New York: Seaview Books, 1979), pp. 419–420.

5. Matthew Josephson, *Edison: A Biography*, rev. ed. (New York: John Wiley, 1992), p. 423.

6. Baldwin, p. 345.

Chapter 8. Becoming a Legend

1. Neil Baldwin, *Edison: Inventing the Century* (New York: Hyperion, 1995), p. 291.

2. Ibid., p. 182.

3. Ibid., p. 189.

4. Ibid., p. 313.

5. Ibid.

6. Ibid., p. 335.

7. Robert Conot, *A Streak of Luck* (New York: Seaview Books, 1979), pp. 434.

8. Baldwin, pp. 389, 398.

9. Conot, p. 434.

10. Baldwin, pp. 396–397.

11. Ibid., p. 407.

GLOSSARY

Allies—In World War I, the association of nations including the United States, the United Kingdom, France, and Italy.

arc—Glowing light of electricity across a gap in a circuit or between electrodes.

bulrushes—Plants that grow in wetlands.

camaraderie—Friendship.

canal—A man-made waterway.

celluloid film—Film used to make motion pictures.

Central Powers—The losing side in World War I, including Germany, Austria-Hungary, Turkey, and Bulgaria.

countrified—Unsophisticated.

dynamo—A machine that changes mechanical energy into electrical energy; a generator.

fraud—The act of intentionally trying to cheat someone.

gables—The triangular end wall of a building.

harness—To make use of.

industry—The activity of manufacturing as a whole.

manufacture—To make.

novelty—Something new or unusual.

obsolete—No longer in use or no longer useful.

overthrow—To bring down or defeat.

papyrus—A plant of the Nile valley in Egypt, used to make paper.

philosopher—A person who seeks wisdom.

phosphorus—A nonmetallic chemical element.

physics—The study of natural science.

platinum—A heavy precious grayish-white metallic element.

reform—Change to make better.

scarlet fever—A severe contagious disease characterized by a red rash and inflammation of the nose, throat, and mouth.

spinal meningitis—A serious disease that affects the membranes covering the brain and spinal cord.

stigma—A mark of shame or discredit.

Treaty of Versailles—Agreement signed on June 28, 1919, that officially ended World War I.

typhoid fever—A contagious disease caused by a bacterium. Symptoms include fever, headache, diarrhea, and inflammation of the intestines.

vacuum—A space completely void of matter.

FURTHER READING

Adair, Gene. *Thomas Alva Edison: Inventing the Electric Age.* New York: Oxford University Press, 1997.

Burgan, Michael. *Thomas Alva Edison: Great American Inventor.* North Mankato, Minn.: Compass Point Books, 2006.

Hakim, Joy. *An Age of Extremes: 1880–1917.* New York: Oxford University Press, 2006.

Price-Groff, Claire. *Thomas Alva Edison: Inventor and Entrepreneur.* Danbury, Conn.: Children's Press, 2003.

Stross, Randall E. *The Wizard of Menlo Park: How Thomas Alva Edison Invented the Modern World.* New York: Broadway Books, 2008.

Tagliaferro, Linda. *Thomas Edison: Inventor of the Age of Electricity,* Minneapolis, Minn.: Lerner Publishing Group, 2003.

INDEX